DEVELOP YOUR FINANCIAL INTELLIGENCE

ENHANCE YOUR FINANCIAL SENSE AND TAKE CONTROL OF YOUR FINANCES

ROSIE BROOK

TABLE OF CONTENTS

INTRODUCTION

Understandably, most of us, if not all of us, yearn and desire something greater. It is entirely up to us if we desire a larger vehicle, a better home, or to purchase upscale items for the family. We continuously yearn for more, but getting what you want means taking a risk or trying something new.

It only means carrying out the same behavior repeatedly while expecting various results!
You cannot continue working at the same place of employment indefinitely and anticipate a sudden raise from your employer. It will be a blessing for you that your employer is not downsizing. Shifting employers will only provide a short-term solution to this issue.

The question is whether you have the time and energy to take on a second or third job.

The bottom line: It is not financially sensible to exchange time for money over the long term. You keep putting in longer hours to win the rat race, but at the end of the day, you are still a rat in the mill!

Only when your income increases does your tax bracket change. Your income increases, but so are your expenses for a house and a car. How will you have any money left over to invest in yourself when you spend all of your time working for a company, the government, and the bank to pay off your house and car?

What if you become sick tomorrow and can't go to work? Will the government provide for your family?
I have significant doubts.

Isn't it time you gave your finances a bit more thought, then?

CHAPTER ONE

BASIS OF FINANCIAL IQ

What Is money?

As you can see, different people have different beliefs about what money is.

Some claim that it is a measurement.

Yes, but what kind of measurement? Wealth? How many cows, lambs, and horses someone owned in ancient times served as a proxy for their prosperity. But are your cows and horses still used as a measure of wealth today? Consider slavery. Was there ever a time when labor was in high demand? Are slaves still valuable today? Will the dollar cash you have in the bank shield you from a recession?

No, a dollar bill cannot be used to quantify wealth. It is allegedly a form of power.

Yes, money can give you power, but will a trillion dollars mean much to you if you are stranded on a desert island for all time? Money is not a reliable indicator of power because you would trade it all in an instant for water and a helicopter to get you out of there (hint!). Instead, power largely depends on how and how wisely you use money.

Many people think it's the source of all evil. and many others adopt this viewpoint without much hesitation.

Now, right now, please Money is NOT the source of all evil (otherwise, why do you think churches still take monetary donations and charitable contributions?) The basis of all evil is a love of money. Always keep in mind that money makes a terrible master but a wonderful servant. Money has control over your time and life if you are selling your life for a single dollar.

Lack of money can also lead to a lot of evil thinking and a bad attitude, as seen most often in cheats, thieves, criminals, breakups, freeloaders, cheapskates, and other undesirable characters. This is especially true if you lack proper financial intelligence.

Yet what exactly is money?

Money is an idea supported by assurance. Money today is essentially invented by the rich and powerful, as opposed to earlier times when it was naturally formed by merchants to replace the dubious barter system.

Entrepreneurs are prepared to spend cash to secure the time of others. The time of employees and independent contractors becomes an advantage for their employers, who use this priceless resource to continue building their own wealth.

The truth is that you are enslaved by money as long as you work for it. 90% to 80% of the world's population is currently being held as slaves.

We are unaware that there is a piece of our soul that cannot be purchased, no matter how much money is spent. If your boss immediately offered you 24 months of your income, would you cut off your little finger? We both agree that we are more valuable than that. However, we can have our eyeballs burst out of our sockets when we learn about incidents when people in other nations sell their body parts for money.

But periodically, just like a donkey and a carrot, we DO trade off a piece of ourselves for cash.

Knowledge Is Key to Change
Don't misunderstand me, though: I'm not a

stickler about having a job (I worked at one before I became an Internet Entrepreneur).

But let's face it, our wants are greater now than they have ever been throughout history. While prices rise, salaries do not. Baby boomers are more prevalent than ever and have a relatively meager pension to show for their decades of labor.

And it's impossible to guess how many people really, truly detest the stressful, unhealthy way of life that involves getting up early, dealing with stress for the majority of the day, sitting in traffic, spending more time and money on travel, getting little sleep, and repeating the vicious cycle.

It certainly doesn't present a favorable picture of one's finances and lifestyle, eh?

Being conscious of the issue is the first step toward change. If you want to start taking control of your financial life and subsequently escape the rat race, you need to start with awareness before change, or ABC for short.

In order to know what state we are in and where we are going, we need awareness. Let's start with a small activity before we close this chapter:

Time and resources

In general, there are four different categories of people in the world:

(1) I have neither the time nor the resources.

The majority of workers fall into this category. You cannot fire your boss at any time or go shopping on a Tuesday afternoon. Most workers aren't even able to save enough for a three-year retirement!

(2) Lots of money, little time.
This category includes professionals, small company owners, and self-employed

people. They are marginally better off than an employee since they make more money, but they have to work even harder to keep up with the competition, shrinking profit margins, and customer service.

(3) Have time but no funds.

Many farmers, peasants, college dropouts, or bums are overworked but underpaid. Perhaps ignorance is bliss, but how long can you survive without a reliable source of income?

(4) I have a lot of time and money.

Big business owners, landlords, and investors fall under this category. Imagine not having to work for money, but rather having money work for you by being invested and generating returns on your investments.

Short test

1. Which of the four categories would you say you fall under right now?

2. Which category do you want to be in the future?

CHAPTER TWO

Methods for Getting Rich

Two Models of Wealth Creation

Everybody wants to increase their income, but most people fall into one of two categories:

Those who deliver achievements after being originally promised wealth

Or

Those that deliver the goods initially are rewarded later on by other people.
Let's examine the two groups in greater detail.

People who act only after being promised large, fat paychecks resemble employees, college freshmen, or mercenaries more.

Although there is no right or wrong with this way of thinking, keep in mind that you are once again exchanging your valuable time for money. You labor on something that is uptemporary, limited in wealth, and does not provide you with income long after you quit working, instead of investing your time in an ASSET that produces income.

Remember that having such restricted or temporary results is the best case scenario for this type of short-term vision.
When the manager is not around, have you ever caught a security guard dozing off at work?
Additionally, when we allow the pursuit of money to rule our life, this is another instance in which our emotions take control. It is obvious that when an employee is offered a larger income, more medical benefits, or longer vacation time, their heart begins to beat more quickly.

Financial difficulties do not necessarily decrease with salary. Instead, as your income rises, so do your responsibilities, your tax bracket, and the amount of time you spend working for your firm. The more money you make, the less powerful you are because if your employer pays you five figures and calls an emergency meeting, you better run over there even if you are halfway making out with your wife!

The best way to describe an employee-boss relationship, in my opinion, is as follows.

A worker will only put forth the barest effort to avoid being fired by their employer, and a manager will only provide the barest compensation to keep a worker from quitting.

Let's investigate the other group now.

This category includes a lot of inventors, business leaders, entrepreneurs, and creative thinkers. Someone who consistently has good ideas is an entrepreneur.

We need to stop working for money as our first challenge if we want to succeed in the second group. Which does this imply? Isn't making money a necessary component of having a high financial IQ?

To stop working for money is not the same as working for nothing. Instead, it implies working to acquire the abilities required to become a successful entrepreneur (or inventor, investor). Let me give you an example:

Where would be the best location to hunt for contacts if you don't have the ones you need to start a business? Of course, the clients of your rivals.

What about product understanding? Then join a business that will instruct you in all the details of the trade's secrets.

Not familiar with a factory's production line? Engage in one! either get experience or oversee the factory employees.

Fear of social interaction? Get a position in sales where you must interact with many people.

It is a fantastic way to practice perseverance as well!

Don't you know that the best education you can get is in real life! not in a classroom.

The truth is that not everyone has what it takes to be a successful entrepreneur.

It's not that simple. Many give up too soon before any results can be seen because they lack the persistence, the creative attitude, the resources, or the people needed to complete the task. Learning such skills firsthand is the quickest way to achieve, and you can be paid while doing it! Do not become preoccupied with your salary.

Their first assignment while Donald Trump was choosing candidates for The Apprentice was to go out and sell lemonade! Many would consider it to be a lowly task. But to The Donald, it was crucial: How on earth can you manage a difficult assignment like running the Trump Empire if you can't even do something as easy as selling lemonade?

Once more, let me be clear:

Would you exchange time for immediate cash? (When you quit, money stops coming in)
Or

Trade your time and money for an asset that will bring you income over the long term? (Even after you have stopped for a while).

God endowed us with mental faculties. We only need to glance around to see obstacles to conquer because every obstacle is actually an opening.

Everything is up to you. Although you might not notice the benefits right away, utilizing our minds and the resources at our disposal, we can generate real value that makes others want to pay for what we have to give.

Three Ways to Make Money

I'll list the three ways to earn money below.

• Employees and self-employed people trading time for money.
• Making & Using Creative Ideas - for programmers, artists, and inventors

• Making use of resources and other people, such as leaders and businesspeople.

Have you considered publishing an e-book about your area of expertise if you are a professional? In place of you selling out your time serving your clients, if it is well written, it could offer a new source of money.

What about a coder for computers? Instead of pitching your ideas to the firm you work for, you could create your own ground-breaking product.

What about real estate? Instead of selling homes, you could pool your resources to buy affordable homes, increase their value, and then sell them for more money. Finding good ideas merely requires a little effort and investigation.

Is money an issue? If you can take the risk, look into financing. Collect funds from numerous investors or look for a grant.

When it comes to earning money, the possibilities are endless.

Once more, how do you plan to become wealthy? Response: It's entirely up to you

CHAPTER THREE

The Most Important Investing Rule

What Do People Mean By Investing?

When you hear the word investing, what comes to mind?
Does that entail investing in high-yield assets, mutual funds, insurance, or even the stock market?
Others might only consider investing when they are going to pass away and have nothing left for their heirs.
Some people even shiver when they hear the word, frequently claiming that they don't have any money to invest or that the topic is too complex to even broach.

Many people spend a lot of money on personal trainers, beauty services, and health supplements in an effort to live longer, be healthier, or even appear younger! Consider the advertising budget that modern beauty companies have.

All of these questions about investing are valid ones, but I'm referring to the most significant investment a person can make in a lifetime.

Invest on yourself

"Invest in Yourself" is the most crucial and fundamental rule since, if you don't, who else will?
Your parents will only make educational investments in you up until you graduate from college. However, this only covers the bare minimum and does not impart any crucial knowledge regarding financial education.

If you needed to learn how to make money, would you rely on schools or universities? Most universities just provide you with the skills necessary to work for others while earning money. What about a business education? If business professors are such accomplished practitioners of the subject, why do they continue to teach there rather than building successful businesses?

Would your boss give you business advice so that you can one day hold his position?

The only person who can assume that duty is you.

You see, investing in oneself entails accepting the value of education for oneself. Not in the academic or technical sense, although those are vital life skills to acquire. After college, our education doesn't end.

After leaving college, the majority of working individuals' education enters a stage of retardation. They cease growing when they stop learning. They only eat too many pizzas or takeout during their hectic lunch breaks, which causes them to sag.

IQ is a significant factor, right? But why aren't the world's wealthiest individuals the world's smartest people? Every evening, a lot of accountants and financial planners rush to their automobiles in an effort to avoid the after-work traffic jams! They are not well off.

How about emotional quotient, or EQ? Do putting in a lot of effort, being cheerful, and having a wonderful attitude really improve our financial situation? These are crucial for managing a firm, however allow me to give an example:

No matter how quickly you drive your automobile (working hard), if you are utilizing the wrong route map to travel from Boston to New York, you won't reach your destination. Work harder, but you'll only move quicker in the wrong direction! Even if you have the world's best attitude or the most optimistic mindset, you still won't be able to travel to New York (although the trip wouldn't upset you because you are feeling optimistic about it).

Financial Education's Vitality

FIRST, you need to develop your financial IQ.

Saving a ton of money or investing it all in mutual funds is not the way to develop a strong financial IQ. It is creating a solid relationship with money and accumulating a wealth of assets that will bring in income.

How do you increase your financial IQ?

One of the key elements of increasing your financial IQ is learning to delay gratification. As an example, consider this.

Which would you rather buy: a cow or a pint of milk?

If you purchase milk, it is finished after it is drunk. When the milk is gone, you will need to get more .Even though the price of the milk is less than the cost of a cow, you will eventually have to keep buying milk.

Now, if the price of a cow were to be 50 times higher than the price of milk, you might spend through the nose to buy the cow, but after drinking 50 pints of milk from the cow, you would break even on your investment and begin to save more money. In reality, the cow may give birth to two or more calves, and you could be able to make money by selling one of them!

Get the picture?

EVERYONE has the capacity to build riches. A beat-up old car could be sold for more money when it has been overhauled, given a fresh coat of paint, and has had a few additional parts changed to get it functioning again. In the process, you would have generated wealth!

Possibly a farm? Wouldn't the value of a farm increase significantly if it were converted into a vacation resort with country homes as accommodations?

The same idea applies to craftsmen, computer programmers, and chefs. The whole is larger than the sum of its parts.

The first step to sparking our creativity is realizing that we are all capable of creating wealth, even out of nothing.
Anything's value is determined by supply and demand.

This may be understood without majoring in economics. Just a concept, money. Recall the example of the desert island? The amount of money is not truly measured in cents or dollars. No

Would people be willing to pay you more than usual if you had created a product that they wanted? Would you use your talents to produce quality assets?

The conclusion is this:
Invest in items that will appreciate over time. An asset is anything that increases your revenue. Don't put too much money into risky investments like boats or cars.

If you lose your job tomorrow and are unable to make your mortgage payment, is your house an asset or a liability? Even houses are not considered assets until they are completely paid off.
Are you prepared to leave your comfort zone and pay the price for financial intelligence, or will you continue to live within your means and never take risks to improve the future of your family in order to rely on your employer, the government, and the bank for financial support for the rest of your life?

CHAPTER FOUR

How to Clean Up Your Financial Situation.

I can suggest two strategies for getting out of a financial struggle:

Defensive Techniques

The opening one is a defense:
Reduce the amount you are already spending. If your finances are in a mess, you cannot launch a business. Revenue is not as crucial as cash flow. And if you want to prosper, you need to have a lot of money pouring in from your own pockets.

Here are some areas where you can cut back.

- If you can't stop smoking, just cut back on a few sticks.

Alcohol - drinking will deplete your savings more quickly than a running faucet

- Going out on the town - spend some nights at home contemplating how to earn more money

- Food - eat healthy and you can even think more clearly.
- Gambling - if you plan to gamble, it is better to gamble in a business.

- Vacation and Country Clubs - you won't die without a few memberships.

The main thing that will hold you back is laziness.

The most crucial thing is to avoid purchasing anything that could become a liability. Anything that drains your bank account, regardless of how much they may be worth in the future, is a liability. Consider the cash flow. What can I invest in right now to generate money tomorrow?

Let's now discuss offensive tactics:

Offensive Techniques

The best and least expensive approach to improve your business skills is to join a Network Marketing organization. Other choices include launching a conventional business or perhaps even an online business.

But in terms of business abilities, network marketing is my recommendation if you want to provide yourself with tangible assurance.

The main reason I would advise everyone to invest in a network marketing company is because of what you can learn there, not because of how much money you can make (although it would be fantastic if you can make a lot of money there). This is true regardless of what you have heard about this industry or how much money people have lost there.

Network marketing organizations are the only places where people will freely divulge their trade secrets. It makes sense because your upline will want you to succeed in order for them to be successful! As a result, they won't hold back when teaching you how to conduct business.

Additionally, the very modest cost of joining a network marketing organization will astound you given how much you can learn for the money you spend (a few vitamin bottles and a starter kit for an unforgettable experience!) The attitudes and business skills you need to succeed in this field will be painstakingly taught to you by them.

Basically, having an employee mentality will not help you thrive in network marketing. Your upline will serve as your personal coach and mentor, and a network marketing organization will train you in sales, communication, teamwork, leadership, positive thinking, and self-improvement. I'll venture to say that even if you didn't make any money but dutifully followed their program, the abilities you gain will be useful for the rest of your life.

By joining an insurance company, you can also advance your career. Even if the work may be difficult, those organizations will teach you the aforementioned skills and perhaps even provide you some advice on financial planning in addition.

Consider starting an online business. Internet enterprises offer a low cost, high profit margin business that can produce a lot of money and access into a global market if you have the technical acumen.

Other sites where you may learn about business skills include time management, real estate investing, and financial planning classes.

These are all the best ways to launch a new company that I can think of. For start-up and schooling, you only need to budget a few hundred to a thousand dollars. Someone with no prior business expertise could find a standard business to be overly dangerous. Tens of thousands of dollars are invested, and you can have trouble breaking even. However, your chances of success will increase once you have mastered the aforementioned qualities.

Aside from having a positive attitude about learning, the people you associate with matter most. You are made up of the five individuals you spend the most time with, as it has been mentioned before.

This is incredibly difficult to accept, but consider what they would say if you told your five beer-drinking, poker-playing buddies that you wanted to strike it rich on your own. They would make you laugh so hard they would cry before destroying your ego!
Jealousy is at the core of the human being. They oppose the success of those in their immediate vicinity. If you are successful, they will seem foolish. They love that

lifestyle despite knowing in their hearts they are doomed to failure and drag you down with them. If you are not careful, they will steal your dream and your financial independence!

The most important thing to bear in mind is to only associate with positive thinkers. Thinking positively is not wishful thinking. A dreamer who doesn't act is a wishful thinker. You will sense the energy of those who believe in you and support your goals because positive thinking is supported by action.
You'll quack if you hang out with ducks... but, you will soar if you associate with eagles!

Therefore, start looking for individuals who are willing to grow alongside you or who will support your idea.
The final step is to **BELIEVE IN YOURSELF.**

CONCLUSION

Many people won't support your dream, and leaving your comfort zone can seem daunting. Even if you don't share their desire, they might even start acting aggressively. Even your spouse or parents could be that person.

You will then have to decide whether your financial freedom is worth the price you are currently paying. Is it possible for me to endure one more day of the same routine, work, income, or slog? If the answer is no, act right away. Not tomorrow; when you awaken, you won't remember your dream.

Your wish should be written down on paper and held close to your heart every day. Share it with a supportive person and take action.

You won't be sorry.

Happy Financial Freedom Day!

www.ingramcontent.com/pod-product-compliance
Lightning Source LLC
Chambersburg PA
CBHW070318240526
45467CB00046B/1985